The
TEXAS SERIES

TEXAS MUSIC

Legends from the Lone Star State

★

by John Morthland

TEXAS MUSIC

Legends from the Lone Star State

by John Morthland

CAPSTONE PRESS
a capstone imprint

The Texas Series is published by Capstone Press,
151 Good Counsel Drive, P.O. Box 669, Mankato, Minnesota 56002.
www.capstonepub.com

Books published by Capstone Press are manufactured with paper
containing at least 10 percent post-consumer waste.

Editorial Credits
Catherine Neitge, managing editor; Tracy Davies and Ashlee Suker, designers;
Svetlana Zhurkin, media researcher; Laura Manthe, production specialist

Library of Congress Cataloging-in-Publication Data
Morthland, John.
  Texas Music : legends from the Lone Star State / by John Morthland.
     p. cm.—(The Texas series)
  Includes bibliographical references.
  ISBN 978-1-4296-6763-0 (hardcover)
  ISBN 978-1-4296-5565-1 (paperback)
  1. Country musicians—Texas—Biography. 2. Rock musicians—
Texas—Biography. 3. Blues musicians—Texas—Biography. I. Title.
ML385.M66 2011
781.64092'2764—dc22 [B]   2010028096

Image Credits
Courtesy of Bob Merlis, 77; Getty Images/Frank Driggs Collection, 27, 31, 37; Getty
Images/Michael Ochs Archives, cover (left and middle), 39, 41; Getty Images/Michael
Ochs Archives/Charlyn Zlotnik, 43; Getty Images/Michael Ochs Archives/Frank
Driggs, 28–29; Getty Images/Redferns/David Redfern, 33, 59; Getty Images/Redferns/
Gilles Petard, 35; Getty Images/Time Life Pictures/March Of Time, 19; iStockphoto/
Elaine Harriott, 7; iStockphoto/Kevin Brown, 2–3; Library of Congress, 9, 21, 22–23,
25; Newscom, 13, 17, 48–49, 53, 55, 63 (bottom), 65, 69, 71, 73, 83, 85, 87, 89, 101, 105;
Newscom/Admedia/Kevin Ferguson, 45, 93; Newscom/AFP, 15; Newscom/AFP/
Gabriel Bouys, 107; Newscom/La Opinion/Aurelia Ventura, 97; Newscom/Lexington
Herald-Leader/David Perry, 95; Newscom/Mirrorpix, 57; Newscom/Pierre Roussel, 99;
Newscom/SHNS/Courtesy MCA Records, 47; Newscom/Sipa Press/Matthew Lauren, 61;
Newscom/Sunshine/StillPhoto Collection, 75; Photo by Dick Cole, Waterloo, Iowa, 51;
Shutterstock/arvzdix, 103; Shutterstock/Ferenc Szelepcsenyi, cover (right); Shutterstock/
Narcis Parfenti, 81; Shutterstock/Steve White Photos, 79; Texas State Library & Archives
Commission, 63 (top); Wikimedia/Andy Newcombe, 11; Wikimedia/Bob Jagendorf, 67;
Wikimedia/Craig O'Neal, 91

Printed in the United States of America in Stevens Point, Wisconsin.
082010
005922F10

TABLE OF CONTENTS

Little Bit of Everything in Texas Music

Though Louisiana and Tennessee might disagree, Texas has got to be the most musical state in the Union. Name a genre or subgenre of popular music, and Texas musicians have made major contributions to the style—if they didn't create it outright. And regional styles from zydeco to conjunto, Tejano, and Czech and German polka have many appreciative fans in the Lone Star State.

Fort Worth native T-Bone Burnett is the thinking person's producer of roots music and a quirky recording artist in his own right. He likes to compare Texas music to places in the Gulf of Mexico where freshwater from the Rio Grande and other rivers joins the saltwater in the gulf, and everything gets all mixed up. Because of Texas' location in the United States, T-Bone says, something like that happens with music too. Sounds from around the country make their way down on radio airwaves and mix with Texas sounds to

Creating wonderful music, Texas-style

create something new and different. Tejanos—Texans of
Mexican descent—have put their stylistic stamp on rock 'n'
roll, country, and other genres. Cajuns in Houston and East

Texas have their own music, which takes from and feeds into country. Their Creole counterparts play zydeco, basically blues that's usually sung in French and has an accordion as the lead instrument.

Texas' role in creating and perpetuating American music can be seen most clearly in the realm of country and western music. The first country record released commercially was the traditional fiddle tune "Sally Goodin," by Eck Robertson of Amarillo. It was cut in New York in 1922 and came out on Victor in April 1923. The first country record to qualify as a monster hit was Vernon Dalhart's "Prisoner's Song," with "The Wreck of the Old 97" on the flip side, a Victor release from 1924. Dalhart, whose real name was Marion Try Slaughter, had gone to New York to become an opera singer. When that didn't work out, he began recording pop and patriotic tunes, then switched to hillbilly, as it was then called, and sold millions.

Robertson and Dalhart represent just the beginnings of the country music industry. Not only did Gene Autry create the singing cowboy and Milton Brown and Bob Wills create western swing, but West Texans Ernest Tubb and Floyd Tillman were the fathers of honky-tonk country. East Texan Jim Reeves is one of the first country singers whose records bore the Nashville Sound. And Willie Nelson and cohorts are responsible for progressive outlaw country.

Texas had blues artists just like the other southern

Vernon Dalhart, first opera and then country

states, but the Texans had their own style of acoustic blues. It grew into a Texas style of electric blues in the 1950s and '60s, thanks to Duke-Peacock Records of Houston. Until Detroit's Motown label came along, Duke-Peacock was the largest black-owned record company in America. Houston was the center for Texas blues, though Dallas and Fort Worth also made major contributions. Today African-Americans in Houston have created a distinctive rap and hip-hop sound. A similar process occurred with rock 'n' roll. In the wake of Buddy Holly and Roy Orbison, then Janis Joplin and ZZ Top,

Texas rockers have tended to keep their music closer to the roots. There's more of a blues or country feel at the heart of most Texas rock than is usually heard in other parts of the nation. Yet Texans have embraced homegrown heavy metal and hard rock that may have left the roots behind entirely.

Thanks to their proximity to New Orleans, Texans were among the first to embrace the birth of jazz. Texans lit up later eras of jazz, right down to the avant-garde sounds that provided the music's stylistic climax. Ornette Coleman, who is still working, is not only one of the fathers of that movement, but also one of the most prolific. And when retro jazz came along as an alternative to the experimental sounds of Coleman and his followers, Texans such as trumpeter Roy Hargrove were in the first wave of musicians to break through.

If Texas musicians from the various genres and subgenres have anything in common, it's that they play a lot of live music. There's never been much of a recording industry in the state. So musicians have always developed their audiences by taking their music directly to the people—in rural dance halls and honky-tonks as well as urban ballrooms and nightclubs—until they've attracted enough attention for the recording industry to come to them. Even after Texans begin making records, they usually continue to put more of a premium on their performing skills— that's where they really prove their mettle. This tendency is inseparable from the historical fact that a lot of Texas music

Ornette Coleman, father of avant-garde jazz

has been dance music. When Lone Star musicians are able to fill the dance floor, they know they're doing their job. There are beloved veteran musicians—such as hot fiddler Johnny Gimble, who was once a Texas Playboy, or singer Johnny Bush, the master of the country shuffle—who have gained household-name status in Texas throughout their careers while having at most a brief impact as recording artists.

As Ernest Tubb once sang, "There's a little bit of everything in Texas." If you really want to see what he meant, check out the kaleidoscopic, mind-boggling range of the state's music. The following artists are a good place to start.

CHAPTER ONE

Gene Autry

Few performers have dominated entertainment media the way Gene Autry did. Autry was a best-selling recording artist and a top-drawing movie star. He had his own radio and TV programs, and he wound up owning a major league baseball team. Autry represents the first, and fullest, flowering of the singing cowboy—one of the most potent, and most heavily romanticized, 20th century American cultural symbols.

Though he was the son of a rancher, Autry was not around during the true heyday of the cowboy. He was born in 1907 in Tioga, near the Oklahoma state line north of Dallas. He was 12 when he began learning guitar, and in 1927 humorist Will Rogers heard Autry singing to himself while working as a telegraph operator on a railroad line in Oklahoma. Rogers encouraged the young man to make singing a career, and for a few years Autry kicked back and forth between the Southwest and New York City. He got his first record deal in 1929 and

Gene Autry and Champion

13

his first hit, "That Silver-Haired Daddy of Mine," three years later. He admired Jimmie Rodgers, and Autry's earliest records copied the Singing Brakeman's popular country and blues fusion right down to the yodeling. Thanks to his sincere, unaffected delivery and his smooth baritone, Autry became the star of *WLS Barn Dance*, a widely heard country radio show broadcast from Chicago. But it was the movies that made him a national icon.

In the early 1930s B-movie westerns were barely hanging on, rendered obsolete by the talkies. Somebody in Hollywood concluded that the way to keep B-westerns alive was to have the cowboys sing. This was a stretch. Real cowboys did way too much hard labor to sing a lot. The few songs they did sing were work songs about cattle punching and the like, set to traditional melodies that everyone already knew. But that Hollywood mogul was onto something—the further the cowboy receded into the past, the greater became the public fascination with the romantic myths of the Old West.

In 1934 Autry went to Hollywood for a small part in the movie *In Old Santa Fe*. He was such a hit that he was immediately signed for a 12-part serial called *The Phantom Empire*, in which he played a version of himself—a gentleman entertainer named Gene Autry who vanquished villains and rode his horse Champion back to the ranch to warble some tunes for the folks in radioland. Like many of the era's westerns, the serial dealt with how the bucolic old ways were

Cover detail of Dell's 1950 *Gene Autry Comics*, vol. 1, no. 40

being threatened by technology and encroaching urbanism. In *The Phantom Empire*, the villains were Muranians, futuristic beings whose civilization was located under Autry's ranch, and whose queen, Tika, had a love-hate attitude toward the star. Some bad guys who'd discovered radium deposits on his ranch were also giving him problems.

America embraced Autry as a leading man, and he quickly made his first Republic Pictures feature, *Tumbling Tumbleweeds*. It was a slightly more down-to-earth story in which our hero solves a murder mystery and sings the title song, which quickly became a western standard. By the time Autry enlisted in the Army during World War II, he was one of the nation's top stars in recording, touring, and moviemaking.

Returning to his career in 1946, Autry started his own publishing company, and he invested heavily in TV and radio stations and real estate. Gene Autry's *Melody Ranch* was a fixture on the CBS Radio Network. "Back in the Saddle Again," its theme, became his signature song. In 1950 he became the first movie star to successfully move to TV, producing and starring in 91 half-hour episodes of *The Gene Autry Show*.

Meanwhile, his records were more popular than ever. His prewar hits, such as "Don't Fence Me In," "South of the Border," and "Blueberry Hill," usually got their western flavor from guitar and accordion and maybe a little steel, but they also used huge violin sections and lush backup choruses in addition to Gene's clear, mellow voice. After the war he tapped into the growing market for children's music and secular Christmas songs with the likes of "Rudolph the Red-Nosed Reindeer." Such Autry songs as "The Yellow Rose of Texas," "Texans Never Cry," and "Deep in the Heart of Texas" have shaped how Americans viewed the Lone Star State.

Then there are the numbers, which have reflected

The singing cowboy at L.A.'s Autry National Center

Americans' view of Gene Autry. He made 640 records—writing or co-writing more than 300 songs. The records sold more than 100 million copies—"Rudolph" was the first record ever to have documented sales exceeding a million copies. He also starred in 93 feature films. That, people, is a superstar.

CHAPTER TWO

Lead Belly

To characterize Lead Belly as a blues artist is to do a grave disservice to the most extraordinary folk musician America has produced. Sure, the man sang some blues—and given that he played acoustic guitar as his primary accompaniment, it's easy to stereotype him—but his legendary contributions are much greater than that. Lead Belly didn't sell more than a handful of records before his death in 1949. But just look at some of his best-known titles and some of the diverse performers who perpetuated them—"Goodnight, Irene" (the Weavers), "Rock Island Line" (Lonnie Donegan and Johnny Cash), "Cotton Fields" (the Beach Boys and Creedence Clearwater Revival), "House of the Rising Sun" (the Animals and Bob Dylan), "Midnight Special" (Johnny Rivers and Jimmy Smith), "Gallis Pole" (as "Gallows Pole" by Led Zeppelin), and "Where Did You Sleep Last Night" (Nirvana). There's not a straight-up blues song among 'em.

Lead Belly and his 12-string guitar, 1937

Born Huddie William Ledbetter in 1889, Lead Belly grew up in black settlements around Caddo Lake, a remote, mysterious, and to this day barely populated area straddling northeast Texas and northwest Louisiana. Since this was the pre-blues era, he learned all the songs of the rich and complex 19th century African-American culture—ballads, string-band music, dance tunes, hollers, work songs, play songs, cowboy ballads, broadsides, spirituals—you name it. At country dances called sukey jumps and other public events, in cotton fields, and on playgrounds, he sang jigs ("Dinah's Got a Wooden Leg"), square dance fiddle tunes ("Green Corn"), children's songs ("Ha, Ha Thisaway"), religious songs ("Get on Board"), and more.

As Lead Belly grew older, he incorporated pop and vaudeville favorites into his repertoire. His "Goodnight, Irene" apparently originated with a racially integrated pop songwriting duo of the 1880s. And as blues came into fashion, Lead Belly, of course, integrated that music into his own. He was, after all, a street singer who had to know a little of everything to win tips from his diverse audience. He learned rags, blues, and boogie forms in the brothels of Shreveport, Louisiana, his first stop after leaving home. With his booming voice and propulsive 12-string guitar work—he never was much for finesse—you'd think he would have made a powerful bluesman, but, with a few exceptions ("Good Morning Blues," "Roberta"), his efforts in that regard are unremarkable compared with his other work.

Yet when Lead Belly made his first commercial recordings in New York City in 1935, all the emphasis was on blues. The record business clearly saw a fearsome black man with a guitar and decided it knew everything there was to know about him and his music. And the story of his past—as shaped by John Lomax, the folklorist who'd brought Lead

Lead Belly and his wife, Martha Promise, 1935

Belly to New York—played nicely into blues stereotypes. In 1915 he'd done time on a Texas chain gang for carrying a pistol. He soon escaped and was living under the name Walter Boyd when he went back to prison in 1918 after killing a relative in a fight over a woman. He was pardoned by Texas Governor Pat Morris Neff —a fan of Lead Belly's singing—after serving the minimum of his seven-to-35-year sentence. In 1930 he was sent to the notorious Angola Prison

Farm in Louisiana for attempted homicide after knifing a white man. That's where John Lomax and his son Alan, who were recording folk songs for the Library of Congress, first encountered him. In 1934, after the Lomaxes took his petition to Louisiana Governor Oscar K. Allen, Lead Belly was again released after serving most of his minimum sentence.

On January 1, 1935, John Lomax and Lead Belly arrived in New York, where the former played the "singing convict"

Lead Belly (foreground) in the Angola Prison Farm, 1934

up to the media, suggesting that the singer's music had won him both his pardons. When he went into the studio, Lead Belly insisted that he record a full range of his material, but only the blues sides were released at the time. They flopped with black Americans, the only blues audience then. Meanwhile, Lead Belly bridled at Lomax's paternalistic management of his life and music, and the two men quickly parted. Lead Belly went back to Louisiana, but he returned to New York in 1936, where he appeared mostly before white folk-music fans. He became a patriarch of that movement, along with men such as Woody Guthrie, who'd lived formative years in the Texas Panhandle town of Pampa.

Despite occasional problems with the law, Lead Belly's career grew, first in New York and then around the country. Reaching way back into his memory, he recorded a staggering variety of music, starred on radio shows, and eventually toured Europe. That 1949 tour was cut short when he was diagnosed with amyotrophic lateral sclerosis— Lou Gehrig's disease—and he died scant months later at age 61. By then the folk music boom was mushrooming, and Bob Dylan's generation was right around the corner.

Huddie William Ledbetter, 1942

CHAPTER THREE

Bob Wills

Bob Wills is one of a handful of true visionaries in American music. He may not have been the creator of western swing—Milton Brown should get credit for that—but over a long career he refined and expanded the style to take it to unimaginable heights. Though he is now known nationally, Wills is still mostly a cult hero outside his native Lone Star State. But within Texas he remains an iconic figure on a level with Sam Houston and Lyndon Johnson. His praises—and his songs—are sung by Willie Nelson, George Strait, Asleep at the Wheel, and countless others.

Born in 1905 near Kosse, southeast of Waco, Jim Bob Wills already had considerable ranch-dance experience as a traditional breakdown fiddler by the time he moved to Fort Worth in 1929. Working first in blackface in medicine and minstrel shows, he soon added blues to his repertoire of breakdowns and waltzes. In 1930 he formed the Wills Fiddle

Bandleader Bob Wills, 1940s

Band, with Milton Brown as vocalist, and that evolved into the Aladdin Laddies. Then, in 1931, they became the Light Crust Doughboys, who advertised the Light Crust Flour of Burrus Mills for future Texas governor W. Lee O'Daniel. Both Wills and Brown were working dances on the side for extra money, which infuriated the autocratic O'Daniel. Brown left the Doughboys in 1932 to form his Musical Brownies, who played many of the popular tunes of the day with a country string band, creating a sound later called western swing. Had he not died following a one-car crash in 1936, there's no telling what Brown might have achieved.

Wills and singer Tommy Duncan, who had replaced Brown, left the Doughboys in 1933 to form a western swing band based in Waco. When Wills moved the group to Tulsa, Oklahoma, the following year, he threw himself into the new sound, hiring drummer Smokey Dacus to power the two-four dance beat and adding horns and jazz piano. Bob Wills and His Texas Playboys, as the band was called, had a regular show on KVOO radio (which called itself the "Voice of Oklahoma") and a residency at Cain's Ballroom in Tulsa.

To keep dancers happy, the repertoire continued to grow until the music was a bold, brassy mix of traditional country fiddle, hot jazz, Mexican motifs, blues, gospel, and pop. It was unlike anything heard before.

The 11-piece band first recorded in Chicago, Illinois, in September 1935. Until torn apart by World War II, the Playboys revisited the studio regularly, cutting the likes of "Steel Guitar Rag" featuring Leon McAuliffe, and the blues song "Sittin' on Top of the World." They created such standards as "Time Changes Everything," "Take Me Back to Tulsa" and, in 1940, "New San Antonio Rose," Wills' biggest pop crossover and a million seller. Guitarist Eldon Shamblin

Bob Wills (on horse, right) and the Playboys, 1945

arrived in 1938 to devise sophisticated arrangements, and a succession of hot fiddlers joined to create the string-band jazz sound while Wills stuck to traditional country fiddle. Wills and the Playboys also toured the Southwest, drawing thousands nightly. It was the Big Band Era, and they were classified alongside the Dorsey Brothers as much as the country acts of the time. They played the part, dressing in sharp, matching western suits. The music was frequently dubbed "western jazz" or "Texas swing," and the band was full of fiery, improvising soloists—Wills hollered and scatted and jive-talked through the songs like a cowboy hipster.

In 1940 and 1941 Wills and the band made movies in Hollywood. In 1942, after several Playboys had quit to join the war effort, Wills enlisted in the Army. He received a medical discharge less than a year later and reformed the Playboys to work out of California. With many of his Texas and Oklahoma fans having relocated there during the war, it proved to be a good decade for him. His band frequently outdrew Benny Goodman, Harry James, and both Tommy and Jimmy Dorsey. Wills could bring in 10,000 a night. *Time* magazine reported that he made $350,000 annually. Though at one point the Texas Playboys numbered 23 musicians, Wills' largest band ever, they were usually smaller, with Wills using electric guitar to replace the full horn section. And his records—"Texas Playboy Rag," "Stay All Night, Stay A Little Longer," "Bubbles in My Beer"— continued to sell. In 1950 Wills cut "Faded Love," which along

Bob Wills (right) and Cajun fiddler Rufus Thibodeaux, 1959

with "New San Antonio Rose," remains his signature song. By then he'd returned to Oklahoma.

Between his debilitating alcoholism, the decline of jazz, and the onslaught of rock 'n' roll, however, Wills faded in the 1950s. He bounced between Texas and California trying futilely to revive his career. Though he continued working until the late 1960s, few country fans outside Texas were aware of the man when Merle Haggard released *My Tribute to Bob Wills* in 1970. The album kicked off a mushrooming western swing revival, and in 1973 Haggard brought together former Texas Playboys to cut the epic *For the Last Time*. A stroke-diminished Wills watched from his wheelchair. Bob Wills died two years later at age 70.

CHAPTER FOUR

T-Bone Walker

As a father of electric guitar music, Aaron Thibeaux "T-Bone" Walker is one of the architects of postwar American popular music. Nearly all the blues that followed his 1940–1955 heyday is built on Walker's sound, and his influence on jazz and rock is just as profound.

Walker wasn't merely one of the first to plug in. He virtually defined how the electric guitar should be played. Nearly all the first wave of electric guitarists—mostly jazzmen such as Charlie Christian, Floyd Smith, and Eddie Durham—came from a region that extended from Houston to Kansas City, Missouri, and the guitarists rose to prominence about the same time Walker did. But all of them tended to regard amplification as a means to make their instrument heard above the rest of the band and noisy nightclub crowds. Walker alone recognized from the beginning that electricity changed the tone and dynamics

Aaron Thibeaux "T-Bone" Walker, 1960s

of the guitar, thus giving the instrument not just a boost in volume but also a completely different sound. Walker's electric guitar swung like no acoustic guitar ever had, creating an element that is still crucial to good blues today. His single-string solos, on which he often phrased like a horn player, led directly to the rock 'n' roll guitar style of Chuck Berry, and then the sounds of such British Invasion greats as Eric Clapton.

How Walker developed his techniques is something of a mystery, for he was never very forthcoming in interviews. Born in 1910 in Linden, he began playing on the streets of Dallas, where he also served as a valet and guide for Blind Lemon Jefferson, the father of Texas acoustic blues. In 1929 Walker cut a single in a style that was basically his interpretation of Jefferson—but he sang in a more urbane style, based perhaps on classic blues singer Ida Cox, with whom he'd also worked. In the early 1930s, besides working with various Dallas-area bands, Walker performed around Texas in medicine shows and behind touring blues stars. He apparently first picked up the electric guitar around 1935, shortly before moving to Los Angeles, California. At first he was as well known there for his dancing as for his musicianship. When he cut "T-Bone's Blues" in 1939 as the front man for Les Hite's Cotton Club Orchestra, he didn't even play guitar—he sang and danced. But the song was a hit, and it gave him a name. In 1942, after an extended residency at Chicago's prestigious Rhumboogie Club, he won a recording contract with Capitol Records, one of a growing number of independent L.A. labels catering to what was then called the "race" market.

The records that followed were the first to fully capture Walker's style—his tone, his dynamics, and his intricate jazz-flavored chording. His guitar sound grew ever more crisp, fluid, and elegant, complementing his mellow, burnished vocals. The style came to be called jump blues, and it dominated black music on the West Coast and throughout the Southwest. Walker made shuffle rhythms the dominant

An acrobatic T-Bone Walker in 1950

dance beat of the day, and put on one of the flashiest and most uninhibited shows ever seen. Dressed in a sharkskin suit, he played guitar behind his back as he did the splits. When he appeared back in his native Lone Star State, he engaged in "Texas Shootouts," guitar duels against such acolytes as Clarence "Gatemouth" Brown. Soon an entire school of guitarists, including Pee Wee Crayton and Lowell Fulson, had formed around the Walker sound.

Walker himself probably peaked in 1946–47, when he recorded for Black & White, another new L.A. "race" label, accompanied by some of the West Coast's classiest jazz and blues sidemen. Among the results were "They Call It Stormy Monday (But Tuesday's Just as Bad)," which became his signature song, one that's been recorded by hundreds of artists since; the landmark "T-Bone Shuffle," which all blues guitarists must know how to play; and "T-Bone Jumps Again," one of his most explosive records. When he switched to Imperial Records in 1950, he came up with the dazzling instrumental "Strollin' with Bone." He menacingly chops the tune into pieces using those downstroked chord passages, and between them he shifts to sharp, piercing lines that he plays as coolly as a man flicking open a switchblade and using it to pick his teeth.

Like many postwar pioneers, Walker could not make a transition to the rock 'n' roll music he helped to midwife, and his career slowed. But he continued recording into the 1970s.

T-Bone Walker in the 1930s; he won a Grammy in 1971

Few of the early and classic rock guitarists failed to cite him as an influence—and whether they know it or not, pretty much all of today's young, rocking electric guitarists have a bite of the T-Bone in their sounds too.

CHAPTER FIVE

George Jones

It's still an open question as to who's the greatest
country music artist—singer, writer, instrumentalist, and
performer—ever. But it probably comes down to Jimmie
Rodgers, Hank Williams, Johnny Cash, or Merle Haggard.
But the greatest singer of all time—despite the fact that
he may be better known for his failed marriages and drug
and alcohol addictions—is an easier call. A widely held
consensus holds that it's George Jones. Even when he's
singing a rare, upbeat lyric, George Jones represents the
sound of pain.

His voice and style are instantly recognizable, yet hard
to describe. The voice, most effective in its middle and lower
ranges, doesn't seem to come from the stomach or throat,
as with most singers. Rather, it seems to start somewhere
in the back of his head, forcing its way out through clenched
teeth. It's as if the heartbreaking truths it conveys were as

George Jones, 1970s

impossible to suppress as they are hard to believe. Words are clipped off or stretched out effortlessly, or transformed halfway through by changes in pitch. Singing mostly ballads, which gives him time to do all this in a single phrase, he creates an effect both devastating and beautiful.

His early style was almost the opposite. Jones was born in 1931 in Saratoga, a lumber town in the Big Thicket, a piney woods region of East Texas that resembles parts of the Deep South. It was a hardscrabble existence, even after the family moved south to Beaumont, where George became a street singer before reaching his teens. In 1953 a Houston wheeler-dealer named Pappy Daily, who became his manager and producer in addition to being the co-owner of his record label, signed him. When "Why, Baby, Why" became Jones' first hit, in the summer of 1955, he was a fairly standard honky-tonk singer, his style a synthesis of Roy Acuff and Hank Williams, with a little Lefty Frizzell thrown in. The high end of his range added a dash of excitement to up-tempo songs like the 1959 moonshining novelty "White Lightning," his first No. 1 country hit. Daily's pointed suggestion that he develop a style of his own initially puzzled Jones, but by 1961 his ballad sound was developing—"Tender Years" rose to No. 1 on a large but smooth production and delicate vocal. Over the rest of the decade, Jones was a steady presence on the charts. While he was signed to Daily's Musicor label between 1965 and 1970, he cut nearly 300 sides.

George Jones sang on the streets of Beaumont

After being overworked like that, he was understandably ready for a change. In 1969, by which time he'd moved to Nashville, Tennessee, he married Tammy Wynette. He switched to her producer and label—Billy Sherrill of Epic Records—in 1971. His first release was a duet with Wynette remaking his 1965 solo hit "Take Me." Sherrill, already famous for his lush "countrypolitan" productions aimed at the mainstream market, pulled out all the stops for both Jones' solo records and the Jones-Wynette duets. The records detailed the ins and outs—and eventually the rise and fall—of their fairy-tale marriage. Amidst real-life stories of Jones' self-destructive ways and Wynette's misfortunes, a whole musical soap opera, complete with Sherrill's banks of strings, played out. It started with Jones' 1972 Epic solo debut "We Can Make It" and ended with the 1974–75 trio of "The Grand Tour," "The Door," and "These Days (I Barely Get By)." The divorce finally came in 1975. Jones went deeper into a tailspin and failed to crack the Top 10 at all from 1976 to 1980. Country fans held their collective breath, waiting for him to annihilate himself in the grand Hank Williams tradition.

Then, in 1980, came the biggest fairy tale yet, and this one endured. The vehicle was "He Stopped Loving Her Today," a tearjerker about a man who, abandoned by his one true love, continued to pine for her until his death. Jones hated the morbid song; he was so wasted while cutting

Tammy Wynette and George Jones sing "Golden Ring"

his vocals that Sherrill had to patch together fragments from countless takes to compile the finished version. But "He Stopped Loving Her Today" was the Country Music Association's Song of the Year two years running. Those who'd been watching and waiting for Jones to die were now declaring him the all-time greatest.

For the rest of the decade, Nashville did all it could to sing Jones' praises. Artists lined up to beg him to legitimize their bland country-pop records by adding his distinctive hard-country vocalisms to them. Jones thrived through the rest of the 1980s and into the '90s. By the turn of the century, after a few failed attempts, he'd even quit drinking. And when the hits stopped coming, he transformed himself once more, this time into a Grand Old Man. He was still the greatest hard country singer ever, everyone agreed, but the marketplace would no longer tolerate hard country. But he still tours as much as he wants to, even without radio airplay, proving night after night that a Grand Old Man is not such a bad thing to be.

George Jones in Nashville, 2004

CHAPTER SIX

Buddy Holly

Buddy Holly was Texas' contribution to the first wave of rock 'n' roll, but he was a whole lot more than just that. In what was basically a three-year career that ended with a famous plane crash in 1959, Holly blazed several important trails that were still being followed generations later.

Like Chuck Berry, he wrote much of his own material. The instrumentation of his band, The Crickets—two guitars, bass, and drums—provided a prototype for countless other bands that followed, including The Beatles. In the studio, Buddy Holly was more or less his own producer, and one of the first to experiment with such electronic wizardry as double-tracking, a technique that let him play or sing along with himself for a fuller sound. At his last session in New York, the kid responsible for tough rockers like "That'll Be the Day" used string sections to orchestrate his maturing ballad sound. He was also one of the first artists to split

Buddy Holly, rock 'n' roll pioneer

with his manager and take over his own business affairs. Buddy Holly was the complete package. And unlike early rockers who exuded danger and rebellion, he was also an All-American boy, an Everyteen whose songs, every one of them about love, reflected the hopes, fears, and uncertainties of the young. With his thick glasses and unaffected manner,

Buddy could easily have been a member of his own audience.

Charles Hardin Holley (the "e" was later dropped from his surname) was born in 1936 in the High Plains town of Lubbock. He took up guitar and piano as a child, and with classmate Bob Montgomery formed his first group, the country duo Buddy and Bob, while in high school. He first

Buddy Holly and The Crickets on British TV, 1958

recorded in Nashville in 1956, where he cut some spirited sides that were a compromise between country and rock and went nowhere. After returning to West Texas, Holly formed a new band, which he took to Norman Petty's studio in nearby Clovis, New Mexico, early in 1957. By now Elvis had taken over pop music, and Holly was ready to rock. Petty encouraged the group to pursue its own sound. Acting as manager, he arranged for a major New York label to release the sides with backing vocals as being by the Crickets and those with double-tracked lead vocal as being by Buddy Holly. Today no such distinctions are made; it's all just Buddy Holly music.

The Crickets' sneering rocker "That'll Be the Day" was the first release, and it shot to No. 1 while selling more than a million copies. It was followed by Buddy's "Peggy Sue," with his hiccupping vocals offset by a rolling beat and his insistent rhythm guitar giving way to trebly leads. The flip of that showed another side of his music. The meditative "Everyday" featured Petty's wife, Vi, on the celeste (a keyboard instrument with a glockenspiel sound) and no drums. The rhythm came from drummer Jerry Allison slapping his knees. The Crickets came back with the frantic "Oh Boy," with a raunchy Bo Diddley beat used for the B-side "Not Fade Away." Though their later records didn't go quite as high on the charts, Buddy Holly and The Crickets were one of the most popular bands on the touring circuit well

Buddy Holly backstage in Waterloo, Iowa, 1958

into 1958. In England they were even more in demand.

In mid-1958 Holly met his wife-to-be, Maria Elena Santiago, who was working at the office of his publisher in New York City, and he proposed to her on their first date. He broke with Petty and in the fall moved into a Greenwich Village apartment with Maria, a big step for a young man from the wilds of West Texas. The Crickets sided with Petty and stayed home in Lubbock. Once he'd settled in, Holly held a session featuring violins, violas, and cellos, which yielded the posthumous hit "It Doesn't Matter Anymore." Demos Holly cut in his apartment with just his acoustic guitar, though not topical songs, suggested he was paying attention to the folk scene then blossoming in the Village. He'd already produced for other singers in Clovis, and he continued doing so in New York. In short, his music and career were all over the place; there was no telling what his future would bring.

The dispute with Petty led to lawsuits and, in need of money, Holly reluctantly assembled a new band and joined the Winter Dance Party Tour in the Midwest in January 1959. After one too many nights on the crowded, freezing tour bus, he and costars Ritchie Valens and fellow Texan J.P. "The Big Bopper" Richardson hired a plane to take them to their next engagement, in Moorhead, Minnesota, after a gig in Clear Lake, Iowa. The plane crashed moments after takeoff, around 2 a.m. on February 3, killing everyone.

Since then, as the significance of his achievements and the durability of his original songs have become more obvious to younger generations, Buddy Holly has grown steadily in stature. Today he's considered part of an elite group that includes Elvis, Chuck Berry, and few others.

Jerry Allison (top), Buddy Holly, and Joe Maudlin, 1955

CHAPTER SEVEN

Roy Orbison

Roy Orbison was one of the most unlikely rockers—if, indeed, he was a rocker at all. His music had none of the African-American influences of most of his peers. His sound was fashioned from white pop and country. Short, shy, and pale, he was hardly noticeable, at least until he took to wearing shades and black clothes all the time. That gave him a look that complemented his brooding songs, with their themes of delusion, loss, and paranoia. He sang them in a magnificent, soaring voice that had a gripping, three-octave range, and he produced them with powerful orchestral effects. Orbison's entire sensibility seemed as apparitional as the West Texas winds he grew up with. Even his fans tended to take him for granted until his 1987-88 comeback sealed his reputation as one of the most durable artists of all time, no matter how you labeled his music.

Born in 1936 in Vernon, Orbison was roughly the same

Roy Orbison between shows in England, 1963

age as the first wave of rock 'n' rollers, though most of them had already faded when he finally hit the big time in 1960. Before that, and despite the 1956 rockabilly hit "Ooby Dooby" for Sun Records, his greatest success had been as a songwriter—most notably for the Everly Brothers, Jerry Lee Lewis, and Buddy Holly. Orbison complained that the music business wanted to sculpt him into a rock 'n' roller, which was not something he felt in his bones. But when he signed in 1959 with Monument Records of Nashville, owner and producer Fred Foster gave him free rein to shape his own sound, and one of the first results was "Only the Lonely." The semi-operatic ballad was co-written with fellow Texan Joe Melson, who was partly responsible for many future Orbison hits. It featured a pronounced, insistent—but not rocking—beat, with piano the closest thing to a lead instrument. As the song builds, a bank of strings riffs out rhythmic emphasis and then settles briefly into a sway. Orbison's lead vocals quaver, to emphasize that nobody knows loneliness the way he does, while Melson's soft backup voice fills out the melody. At the climax, all the other instruments and singers fall out as Orbison modulates up into a startling falsetto that seems to seal his doom.

For the next five years, hits like that just kept coming. Orbison set some of them to Latin rhythms ("Running Scared)," others to rigid, martial beats ("It's Over"), while "Leah" had a percussive Caribbean feel. Some relied on a soft backup voice, while others ("Blue Bayou") used large backing choruses. The melodies were intricate and the structures even more intricate. "In Dreams" had seven distinct movements, which emulated the progression of going to sleep, falling into dreams, and then waking up. Many, like "Running Scared," had no chorus, just a series of verses that built to a climax.

John Lennon (left) celebrates Orbison's 28th birthday, 1964

"Candy Man," with a harmonica leading the way,
sounded like bluesman Jimmy Reed trying to sing folk-rock.
And Orbison's insecurities were always right up front. In
"Running Scared" he fantasizes that his girlfriend is leaving
him and then breathes a sigh of relief when she doesn't. "Oh,
Pretty Woman," his last megahit, turns on a similar flight
of paranoia. "Leah" is a death fantasy that turns out to be
a dream. As Orbison explained in "In Dreams," only in that
state can he attain true happiness.

The American hits stopped when Orbison left Monument, though he remained hugely popular in Europe. His personal life seemed to make real the worst fears of his songs. His wife, Claudette, died in a 1966 motorcycle wreck. While Orbison was on tour in England in 1968, his house burned down and his oldest two sons, trapped inside, were killed. The singer soldiered on, mostly overseas, until the 1980s, when recognition in America swelled into a tsunami. The Eagles hired him as an opening act; Van Halen made "Oh, Pretty Woman" a hit again, as did Don McLean with "Crying;" Orbison won a Grammy for a duet with Emmylou Harris. In 1987 everything came together. Against Orbison's wishes, film director David Lynch used "In Dreams" in an over-the-top scene from his cult classic *Blue Velvet*. Bruce Springsteen inducted Orbison into the Rock and Roll Hall of Fame, then helped to organize an Orbison concert with other contemporary stars that became a TV special. Bob Dylan, Jeff Lynne, Tom Petty, and George Harrison anointed Orbison the patriarch of their ad hoc group the Traveling Wilburys, who immediately cut a hit album and single. The album was riding high on the charts when Orbison died of a heart attack late in 1988. His recently completed solo album, *Mystery Girl*, was released posthumously, and it peaked at No. 5 while yielding the No. 9 single "You Got It." Roy Orbison, the singer's singer, went down singing.

Roy Orbison won five Grammy awards

CHAPTER EIGHT

Willie Nelson

In Texas Willie Nelson can do pretty much whatever he darn well pleases. He can appear before a dressy audience of neatly coiffed and well-groomed men and women when he is wearing jeans and a T-shirt and has hair down to his butt. He can proselytize for marijuana use. He can run up a $17 million tab with the Internal Revenue Service and lose everything he owns in a government auction, only to see it bought and returned to him by a wealthy rancher fan. He can cut albums of reggae, record with totally incompatible bands such as Aerosmith, and cut duets with hopelessly unhip partners like Julio Iglesias. Texans of all classes, types, and lifestyles unite in their love for Willie Nelson because Willie is Us—the personification of 20th century Texas as it moved from rural to urban, from cowboys and oil wildcatters to tech nerds, from folk culture to mass culture. The Grateful Dead may have sung of a "long, strange trip," but Nelson lived it, and still does.

Willie Nelson performs at Farm Aid, 2007

Born in 1933 in Fort Worth, Willie was raised with his sister Bobbie, who later became his pianist, by their grandparents 60 miles south in the small farm town of Abbott. He grew up playing in country and polka bands and kicked around central Texas, with stints in the military and in Vancouver, Washington, before moving to Nashville in 1960. He wrote "Family Bible," which became a hit for Claude Gray, and Nelson planned to parlay that into a career of his own. His first successes, though, were more hit songs for others—"Night Life" (Ray Price), "Hello Walls" (Faron Young), "Funny How Time Slips Away" (Billy Walker), and "Crazy" (Patsy Cline). Even after he got a contract, Nelson's records sold disappointingly. The Nashville production methods that were forced upon him gutted and homogenized his distinctly craggy, monochromatic voice and unusual way of singing behind the beat. Nelson grew more disillusioned with the system throughout the decade. When his house burned down in 1970, he moved back to Texas.

At Austin's huge music hall, the Armadillo World Headquarters, he built an unlikely new scene that united the redneck country audience with hip young fans who'd grown up on country but left it for rock. Nelson ignored the overworked formulas that usually spelled country success and instead made music that combined country's earthiness with rock's self-expression. He dressed down, grew his hair long, and got funky. But Nelson still needed a record

Willie Nelson sings at the Texas Prison Rodeo, 1975

Cover of Nelson's *It Always Will Be* album, 2004

breakthrough to spread progressive country, as it was being dubbed. That came with the 1975 concept album *Red Headed Stranger* and its hit single "Blue Eyes Crying in the Rain." Both bore such a skeletal acoustic sound that his label didn't want to release them at all, but Nelson had already gotten himself a rock-savvy manager who'd won Nelson the artistic freedom to create his own sound. The album and single came out as recorded, enjoyed unprecedented crossover sales, and broke Nashville's stranglehold on its artists. Nelson was suddenly the leader of an outlaw movement that included West Texan Waylon Jennings, whose own singular style had been sabotaged by Nashville producers for years. Nelson had beaten the system to become perhaps the most unmistakable voice in American music.

After that there was no stopping him. In 1978 he released *Stardust*, an album of Tin Pan Alley standards that had little to do with country or rock, and that defied all conventional wisdom. The album stayed on the charts for the next decade, and Nelson graduated from country star to American icon. He toured the nation and the world seemingly nonstop, cranking out raucous, two-hour shows with his Family Band that were full of surprises. His annual 4th of July Picnic became an institution for experimental and traditional country music. His records were all over the map—tributes to heroes from Lefty Frizzell to Kris Kristofferson, duets with Jennings, gospel music, more song-cycles and concept albums, and grab bags of songs he liked that didn't fit anywhere else. In 1979 he appeared in the Robert Redford-Jane Fonda film *Electric Horseman*; in 1980 he starred in *Honeysuckle Rose*, for which he wrote the No. 1 hit "On the Road Again."

Willie Nelson on the Strip in Las Vegas, 1980

Though the early '80s was the time of his commercial peak, Nelson enjoyed continuing success while remaining his own man. In 1985 he launched Farm Aid, an annual festival to raise funds for independent farmers. He cut duets with a dizzying array of singers he'd long admired, from Ray Charles to Merle Haggard, and a few that left outlaw fans scratching their heads. He worked with Kristofferson, Jennings, and Johnny Cash in an ad hoc group called The Highwaymen. He fell into a pattern. He'd make albums that were more or less mainstream and contained sure hit singles that'd help keep his career alive. These were followed by some so off the wall that they had no discernible commercial potential but were what he felt like doing at the time.

He's still running his life and his career that way. Who among us wouldn't, if we could get away with it?

Nelson's Farm Aid has raised money and awareness.

CHAPTER NINE

Janis Joplin

Janis Joplin wasn't just a breath of fresh air when she emerged in the popular music world in the mid-1960s. She was more like a whirlwind. She didn't so much sing songs as rip them apart, holding up the pieces to show her own hopes, pleasures, angers, and disappointments. As an iconic figure in the hippie movement—arguably the only woman to hold that position—she represented bundles of contradictions. She was a great singer, but it was the naked emotion she unleashed that awed audiences. She did things her own rebellious way, yet she craved approval. She stood for unlimited freedom, a life with no restrictions, even though her entire persona confirmed that she fully understood there was no such thing. There had been no one like Janis Joplin before her, and none has appeared since her 1970 death of a drug overdose. She commanded your attention like an open wound.

Janis Joplin in concert, 1969

She was born in 1943 and raised in a classic American family in Port Arthur, an oil-refinery town on the Gulf of Mexico. A plain Jane with few friends and lots of arty inclinations in a working-class town that prized conformity, Janis didn't fit in. By the time she finished high school in 1960, she had a reputation for drinking, sexual promiscuity, foul language, and a beatnik appearance. She found solace in her art and in folk music and blues. For several years she tried college, in neighboring Beaumont and in the state capital of Austin, where she was cruelly voted the ugliest girl in her class. But she found a semblance of a peer group in the emerging national countercultural movement. From 1963 to 1965, she lived in San Francisco, singing in coffee houses and experimenting with drugs. After getting too deep into her vices, she returned to Port Arthur and gave the straight life another try. It still didn't suit her at all, and in 1966 she took up an invitation to audition for one of San Francisco's new psychedelic rock bands, Big Brother and the Holding Company.

In keeping with the times, Big Brother was loud, chaotic, and willing to try almost anything. Joplin fit right in as "one of the guys." Her bluesy singing talents blossomed against the speedy attack of the four-man band, with its two wailing guitars and its walls of feedback, distortion, and atonality. Joplin had a harsh voice made more so by her steady ingestion of Southern Comfort. While she could sing as tunefully as the best of 'em—"Summertime" was one of her showstoppers—her strength was in the way she could abandon that to break into knowing chuckles, heart-breaking sighs, vexing questions, desperate moans, or hair-raising screams, all while stomping her foot and shaking her booty. Big Brother was perhaps the most outrageous, unpredictable band in San Francisco. Joplin, in her gaudy stage clothes, glitzy jewelry, and flamboyant, feathery hairdos, rode that wave as if she were born to it.

Big Brother stunned the Monterey Pop Festival in 1967.

Janis Joplin performing in California

Most of the East Coasters there, including the heavies of the music business, had never seen Joplin or the band before. Almost instantly there was a new, big-time record contract with Columbia, a new, big-time manager in Albert Grossman, who handled Bob Dylan, and a lot of lowdown gossip and speculation that maybe Big Brother was, you know, perhaps too inept for such an unpolished jewel of a singer. Though nobody seemed to consider that polishing the jewel could destroy what was unique about it, the talk eventually tore Joplin away from Big Brother to pursue a solo career.

As her stardom grew, so did her insecurities—which meant, of course, that her drinking and drug-taking did too, not to mention her exhibitionism. Her once-spectacular live shows seemed to grow into a spectacle of a different sort, in which she used her music to wallow in her pain. She seemed unable to find lasting pleasures anywhere. *I Got Dem Ol' Kozmic Blues Again, Mama!*, her debut solo album, was a rather safe and sterile attempt to make a soul album with a horn band; she often oversang badly. But she was more popular than ever, as if her audience wanted her to make a human sacrifice of herself, and she couldn't see any way out of that bind.

Still, Joplin seemed to be groping toward a way out before she died. Outwardly she appeared to be gaining more control of her life; she was even engaged. And she

Janis Joplin at the height of her fame in 1968

seemed to be gaining more control over her music. *Pearl*, the album she'd almost finished when she took a fatal shot of heroin, was done with her handpicked combo. On tracks like "Me and Bobby McGee," which eventually became her biggest hit ever, Joplin curbed her excesses while refining her approach, as if she were in it for the long haul. Even her once-potent sense of humor was returning.

We'll never know where she might have been able to go from there, but we do know that during her meteoric time in the spotlight she changed the way the world viewed female musicians.

Janis Joplin at Woodstock in 1969

CHAPTER TEN

ZZ Top

No rock band in history has stayed together as long, with its original personnel, as ZZ Top. "The Little Ol' Band from Texas," as it was known, was formed in 1969, when guitarist Billy Gibbons, formerly of Houston psych favorites Moving Sidewalks, recruited bassist Dusty Hill and drummer Frank Beard, the onetime rhythm section for American Blues in Dallas. To this day they are the only three men who've ever been members of the band. Yet there have been two ZZ Tops.

ZZ Top Number 1 ran from the trio's inception until 1979. ZZ came into this world as a rootsy, hard-rock power trio in the mold of Cream. Like most arena-rockers of the era, they relied heavily on volume, though it was clear from the beginning that Gibbons was a blues-rock guitarist to watch. Their albums, produced by manager Bill Ham, who had a reputation for running their career with an iron

Frank Beard (from left), Billy Gibbons, and Dusty Hill

fist, were sludgy, and it took a while for ZZ to distinguish itself from the pack. Indeed, the band stuck close to home at first. They played Texas far more than anywhere else, while recording in an East Texas studio, and their songs increasingly adapted Lone Star bad-boy themes.

The turning point came in 1973. The band opened shows for the Rolling Stones in Hawaii and recorded *Tres Hombres,* its third album, in Memphis. The album contained "La Grange," about an infamous bordello near their Houston home that also inspired the Broadway musical *The Best Little Whorehouse in Texas.* It was their second, and biggest, hit, and the group began introducing the rest of the nation to Texas ways. In 1974 ZZ Top's First Annual Texas-Size Rompin' Stompin' Barndance and Bar-B-Q, which also featured Santana, Joe Cocker, and Bad Company, drew tens of thousands to Austin. The trio mounted an extensive international tour in 1976 with a stage set that included live snakes, cattle, and bison, as well as cacti and other symbols of Texas. The band had arrived, but it still had little cachet outside the youthful hard rock and metal audience.

ZZ Top Number 2 changed that. After the Texas-themed tour, the trio took three years off. When they returned in 1979, Gibbons and Hill had beards flowing to their waists and Beard sported a moustache. Instead of jeans and western shirts, they usually wore sunglasses and black clothing. *Deguello,* their new album, featured a more nuanced brand of blues-rock, while Gibbons' guitar lines were clean and carefully articulated. On some tracks there was also a saxophone trio made up of Hill, Beard, and Gibbons. These guys were more than a rock-'em-sock-'em big noise—they were musicians. Secure in their Texanness, they began writing such songs as "I'm Bad, I'm Nationwide," while hit singles, such as "Cheap Sunglasses," put aside the bathroom

The bearded look has been going strong since 1979

humor for a more knowing brand of wit. And that was just the beginning. The music on the 1981 album *El Loco* was made in part by a synthesizer, and there were other electronic effects, though the ZZ Top ethos lived on in such laff-riot tunes as "Tube Snake Boogie" and "Party on the Patio."

Eliminator, released in 1983 and still ZZ's biggest album, completed the makeover. While the boys strutted their stuff on "Gimme All Your Loving," "Legs," "Sharp Dressed Man" and "Bad Girl," the sound relied heavily on a synthesizer, as well as other new effects. Beard drummed to a metronomic click track, and suddenly the minimalist, roots-rock power trio was a modern electronics-oriented band.

ZZ was perhaps the first old-line rock band to grasp the potential of then-new MTV. Rather than reluctantly crank out joyless videos because they felt they had to, the guys gleefully used the form to establish their persona and to reinforce the cartoonish bent of the music. It was probably the stylized videos for "Gimme All Your Loving," "Legs" and "Sharp Dressed Man," more than the music itself, which made those songs hits. The videos featured a cherry red 1933 Ford Coupe hot rod dubbed The Eliminator playing a prominent role amid scantily clad babes and the heroic triumvirate of Billy, Dusty, and Frank. The Eliminator became the band's symbol for years to come.

Since then ZZ has had ups and downs, and even another lengthy hiatus. The sound at first grew more electronic,

ZZ Top performs in Bucharest, Romania, 2009

but has since veered back to the blues-rock basics. Sales stayed high, then tapered, and now fluctuate, as does the size of live audiences. The manager who shaped the group's early approach so extensively that he was virtually a fourth member is no longer involved. But the comedy and the guitar acrobatics are still there, along with the forever-youthful celebration of bad girls and good times. That's what seems to keep ZZ Top going.

CHAPTER ELEVEN

Stevie Ray Vaughan

Texas has produced many great singers and instrumentalists in all genres of music, but guitarists —well, guitar players in the wake of T-Bone Walker— just seemed to proliferate. Stevie Ray Vaughan may well represent the culmination of a half-century-plus of electric string-bending: the Last Guitar Hero. Other exceptional guitarists have surfaced in Texas and elsewhere since the Dallas native's death in 1990. But it was Vaughan who summed up so much that had been done with the instrument—mixing the best of several generations of blues whizzes, lacing that with rocking variations from the likes of Eric Clapton and especially Jimi Hendrix, and creating the definitive blues-rock electric guitar sound. Since Stevie Ray Vaughan was silenced, everything that's followed has seemed more like reiteration than like breaking fresh ground.

Stevie Ray Vaughan won four Grammy awards

It was Vaughan who took the fat tone of Albert King and other southern and Chicago bluesmen and ran it through the most powerful modern amplification to create a muscular, hard-edged sound of abrasive chords broken up by frenzied flurries of notes. Vaughan played rhythm and lead simultaneously—a no-nonsense wall of sound. He did this at a time when synthesizers and the style of early MTV were taking over music, and the guitar was falling out of favor. He not only helped return the six-string guitar to prominence but also kicked off the blues revival of the 1980s. And all the while he was sinking into and then overcoming hellish drug and alcohol addictions. He achieved his greatest musical heights following his rehabilitation, only to die in a helicopter crash just when it seemed he was on top of the world.

Older brother Jimmie Vaughan introduced Stevie to both guitar and to postwar electric blues and R&B. Many still argue that Jimmie was the better guitarist. In 1971 Stevie followed Jimmie from their working-class Dallas neighborhood to Austin, where there was greater affinity for white boys lost in the blues. Jimmie scored as a guitarist for the Fabulous Thunderbirds, while Stevie honed his chops in a succession of local bands. Slowly he was carving his own intense, ferocious guitar sound out of such blues influences as Albert King, Buddy Guy, Otis Rush, and Guitar Slim. At the end of the decade, he introduced the final element when

Vaughan is a member of the Blues Hall of Fame

he incorporated the electronic wizardry of Jimi Hendrix and began performing several Hendrix songs. Nobody at that time dared mess with the hallowed Jimi's music, but Stevie did so with his own flair and made it work. He'd also begun singing. Early in the 1980s his group Double Trouble had shrunk to a power trio. Drummer Chris Layton and bassist Tommy Shannon gave Vaughan plenty of room for extended guitar improvisations, which he welcomed by adding a touch of jazz to the mix. He was now the complete front man.

But it was 1982 before he broke out of Texas. That was when he was invited to play the venerable Montreaux Jazz Festival in Switzerland, which was unprecedented for an unknown rocker. There he was seen by David Bowie, who invited Vaughan to play guitar on *Let's Dance*, Bowie's commercial breakout album, and by Jackson Browne, who gave him free time in his studio to record demos that would become Vaughan's debut album. The Rolling Stones hired Vaughan to play a party in New York around the same time. This flurry of big-name endorsements led to a record deal and, in 1983, the release of *Texas Flood*, named after a dramatic slow blues number that was a staple of Vaughan's live set. The album quickly went gold while climbing to No. 38 on the pop charts, which was unheard of for a blues album.

But Vaughan's self-destructive ways grew along with his fame over 1984's scorching *Couldn't Stand the Weather* and 1985's *Soul to Soul*. The albums sold well, though the music lacked his usual fire. When *Live Alive* came out in 1986, the truth was inescapable—the man who had saved blues and guitar rock was now recycling his sure-thing licks by rote, without emotion or imagination. Soon after falling off a stage in 1987, he cut short a European tour and returned to the States to enter drug rehab.

He worked at rehab with the same commitment he'd initially brought to his music. Once clean, he began touring

Vaughan's favorite guitar, a Fender Stratocaster

and preaching the Alcoholics Anonymous gospel of sobriety. The 1989 *In Step*, featuring the ethereal instrumental "Riviera Paradise," was arguably his greatest album, and it went platinum almost overnight. He also cut *Family Style* with brother Jimmie. Stevie Ray Vaughan's last gig was August 26, 1990, at Alpine Valley in southern Wisconsin. He blew headliner Eric Clapton off the outdoor stage and then illuminated an evening-ending jam with Clapton, soul-bluesman Robert Cray, and special guests Buddy Guy and Jimmie Vaughan. Afterward, the helicopter that was supposed to take Stevie through the dense fog back to Chicago crashed into a hillside minutes after takeoff, and one of pop's greatest redemption stories came to an abrupt and shattering end.

Stevie Ray Vaughan was 35 when he died.

CHAPTER TWELVE

George Strait

He's the good-looking, soft-spoken, aw-shucks gentleman in the cowboy hat, the one whose honeyed voice oozes sincerity, empathy, and emotion. George Strait, who has a spotless image and a string of hit records longer than I-10 between Beaumont and El Paso, seems way too good to be for real.

But his history says the South Texan definitely is for real. Since the single "Unwound," his first hit, in 1981, Strait's consistency has been truly amazing. His look and image—Resistol hat, starched western-style shirt, creased Wranglers, polished Justin boots, the quintessential modern cattleman's look—hasn't changed at all, except when he dons a western-style suit or tux for a special event. His sound has changed only slightly. And over a 30-year period during which country music has seen a multitude of trend-setters, overnight sensations, and flavors of the month come and go, his success has stood firm. In 2010 he became

George Strait produces hit after hit.

the first artist to have enjoyed Top 10 hits every year for 30 years in a row; he had 82 such singles in all. Since 1982's "Fool-Hearted Memory," his first No. 1 single, he has racked up 57 more chart-toppers to go along with 33 platinum albums. His annual tours still break box-office records. All of this makes Strait the living embodiment of a favorite Texas expression, "If it ain't broke, don't fix it."

Born in 1952 in Poteet, Strait grew up on a brush-country ranch south of San Antonio that had been in his family for a century. George was raised mostly by his father, a middle school teacher and rancher. After a brief fling with college, he enlisted in the Army in 1971 and spent most of his time in Hawaii playing in an Army country band. After being discharged, he returned to his studies at Southwest Texas State University (now known as Texas State University) in San Marcos, earning a degree in agriculture in 1979. While there he joined with other students in a country group called the Ace In the Hole Band. They were local favorites who caught the eye and ear of club owner Erv Woolsey, who was connected with the Nashville music business. Woolsey felt the group had less of a shot than Strait did as a solo act, and that's how Strait alone was signed to a major Music City label in the early 1980s. He kept the Ace In the Hole name for his backing band, and some of the original musicians stayed with him as well; they still play behind him today.

Fans at a Texas concert show their love for Strait.

Strait built his sound on honky-tonk and western swing, two styles that originated in Texas and persevered there long after national trends had changed. But he never embraced the neon glare and dubious nightlife usually at the heart of that ethos. His music goes down easy, with none of the rough edges of classic honky-tonk. And with very few exceptions—such as "Amarillo by Morning," the 1983 rodeo song many consider his best—his music has obsessively explored the nuances of love and ignored other subjects.

The titles alone tell the story—"You Look So Good In Love," "Right or Wrong," "Does Fort Worth Ever Cross Your Mind," "All My Exes Live In Texas," "Famous Last Words of a Fool," "Love Without End, Amen," "Chill of an Early Fall," "Check Yes or No," "One Night at a Time," "I Just Wanna Dance with You," "She Let Herself Go," "It Just Comes Natural." Female fans swoon over his stance. Even in the weepers, women come off nearly unblemished. Sure, sometimes things don't work out, but it's not because she was a two-timer or back-stabber or anything like that; it's because, well, sometimes things just don't work out, and the pain he feels is usually tempered by the warm feelings that remain. He's a gentleman all the way. He's also what's called a song man—all of his hits are immaculately crafted, with unforgettable melodies and hook-phrases. Strait writes rarely, but he doesn't need to; the top writers in Nashville vie to have him cut their songs.

Because Strait gives almost no interviews, he's never really put his booted foot in his mouth in public. His seemingly stable family life—he married his high school sweetheart—appears to confirm that he means what he's singing. He even still rides and ropes and sponsors a team roping competition. He retains the traditional

George Strait and his wife, Norma

rancher values of chivalry, morality, fair play, and rugged individualism. The reason Texans still embrace George Strait without reservation is that he's the closest thing we have in these increasingly confusing times to an unambiguously good-guy hero. Which, it turns out, the rest of America still seems to like just as much.

And the Musical List Goes On

Perhaps the most amazing thing about this list of a dozen Texas music legends is that there's plenty more where they came from. Texas is a big state with a long and rich history, and this is perhaps truer in music than in other areas. We've barely scratched the surface here.

Starting with the early days of rock 'n' roll and proceeding into the psychedelic era, the cavalcade also includes such big-name performers as 1950s novelty singer J.P. "The Big Bopper" Richardson (Beaumont), rockin' writer/singer Bobby Day (Fort Worth), balladeer and L.A. doo-wop cornerstone Jesse Belvin (San Antonio), 1960s rockers The Bobby Fuller Four (El Paso), folk-pop singer Trini Lopez (Dallas), Tex-Mex garage bands Sam the Sham and the Pharaohs (Dallas) and Question Mark and the Mysterians (south Texas/Mexico), Chicano R&B stars Sunny and the Sunliners (San Antonio), blue-eyed soul man Roy Head, San Antonio rockers The Sir

Trini Lopez

Douglas Quintet, Dallas blues-rockers Steve Miller and Boz Scaggs, psychedelic pioneers 13th Floor Elevators (Austin), and blues-rock guitar hero Johnny Winter (Beaumont), whose brother Edgar became a 1970s arena-rock star.

Most of these musicians had to leave Texas to make it, but the Lone Star State never left their music entirely. That trend has continued, to varying degrees, to this day, via Austin's Butthole Surfers in punk, Austin's Joe King Carrasco in new wave, Dallas' Edie Brickell and the New Bohemians and Gary Myrick and the Figures in post-punk rock, Arlington's Pantera, featuring guitar whiz Dime Bag Darrell, and San Antonio's Pariah in hard rock and metal. And there's the never-ending procession of singer-songwriters coming out of Austin under the Americana label, from Lubbock natives Joe Ely, Butch Hancock, and Jimmie Dale Gilmore to vagabond singer Lucinda Williams and Fort Worth native James McMurtry. Houston has produced its own school of singer-songwriters in Guy Clark, Townes Van Zandt, and Lyle Lovett, and Austin continues to turn out contemporary rock bands, from the veteran Alejandro Escovedo to the artsy ... and You Will Know Us by the Trail of Dead and the indie/alt Spoon.

Texas blues probably began with Blind Lemon Jefferson of Dallas, who proved nearly as vital to the music's future as the fabled Mississippi Delta bluesmen. East Texan Henry Thomas was one of the most enduring pre-blues musicians, while in the 1960s Mance Lipscomb (Navasota) proved the

Clarence "Gatemouth" Brown

last living embodiment of those songsters. Victoria Spivey
and Sippie Wallace (both of Houston) were among the
most popular of the more urbane classic blues singers of
the 1920s. Among the guitarists immediately following in
T-Bone Walker's wake were Pee Wee Crayton of Rockdale,
Oklahoma native Lowell Fulson, whose style was shaped
in Texas, and Clarence "Gatemouth" Brown of Orange, who

ended his career as a multi-instrumentalist playing country, blues, and bluegrass. But the lineage also includes Houston-bred modernists Johnny "Guitar" Watson, Albert Collins, and Johnny Copeland. Postwar jump pianists/singers include Little Willie Littlefield of El Campo and Houston's Amos Milburn, while singer/pianist Charles Brown (Texas City) helped invent mellow cocktail blues. Singer/writer Percy Mayfield, with his haunting music, may have been born in Louisiana, but he spent his formative years in Houston before heading to L.A. The career of Galveston's Esther Phillips began in the jump blues and R&B era and evolved through a variety of genres. In the 1960s Memphis native Bobby "Blue" Bland, the commercial backbone of Duke-Peacock Records, was constantly on the charts singing his Houston-bred, jazz-inflected soul-blues, while guitarist Freddie King (Gilmer) combined the best of Texas and Chicago. Lightnin' Hopkins first emerged from Houston as a jump bluesman, but he switched to solo acoustic performing as the folk era heated up, and eventually he became the most recorded Texas bluesman ever. Today Orange native and New Orleans-style pianist/singer Marcia Ball best represents the Austin legacy of Stevie Ray and Jimmie Vaughan and the Fabulous Thunderbirds.

In the post-blues era of African-American music, Texas has produced soul stars Joe Tex of Navasota and Archie Bell and the Drells from Houston. Though he also led his

Smooth-singing Barry White

own groups, Fort Worth's King Curtis was that rarest of musicians—a star sideman who blew rip-snorting tenor sax solos on everything from Coasters novelties in the early days of rock 'n' roll to Aretha Franklin soul serenades. Sly Stone, a pioneer of psychedelic soul and funk with Sly & the Family Stone, may have come of age in the San Francisco Bay Area, but only after being born and singing in his church choir in Dallas. Barry White, one of the architects of disco, hails from Galveston. The deep, dark sound of Houston has always been crucial to the world of rap and hip-hop, from old school stars the Geto Boys to reigning kingpin Chamillionaire. Meanwhile, the Space City's Beyonce Knowles—and her previous group Destiny's Child—is the queen of contemporary R&B, though Erykah Badu of Dallas is the most fascinating artist the genre has produced.

Texans have been equally influential and equally successful in the realm of African-American gospel music. Slide guitarist/singer Blind Willie Johnson (Brenham) is the acknowledged genius of the street-corner singing evangelists of the 1920s. His music was revived by everyone from Bob Dylan to Led Zeppelin and White Stripes. Arizona Dranes (Sherman) is considered the first gospel pianist. The mid-century Golden Age of the Gospel quartet yielded the Soul Stirrers (Trinity) and the Pilgrim Travelers (Houston). Yolanda Adams (Houston) and Kirk Franklin (Fort Worth) are two of the biggest stars of today and have sold millions of records.

Some of the state's most popular regional stars hail from ethnic and tradition-oriented music. In zydeco, Clifton Chenier was from Louisiana but he worked in Houston and Port Arthur for much of his career. More recently Lil Brian Terry and the Zydeco Travelers (Baytown) created zydeco rap. "Little" Joe Hernandez (Temple), whose career began in 1954 and continues today, is the godfather of Tejano, the Chicano form of pop music, while the martyred

Beyonce Knowles

Selena (Corpus Christi) was the biggest Tejano star ever.
The best-known name in conjunto, the accordion-fueled,
Tex-Mex traditional sound, is San Antonio's Flaco Jimenez,
who's worked with Dwight Yoakam and the Rolling Stones.
Avant-gardist Steve Jordan (Elsa) and San Antonio's Mingo

Saldivar and Eva Ybarra have also enjoyed crossover success. The Texas Tornados blew out of San Antonio in the 1990s as a Tex-Mex supergroup. Flaco and San Benito's Freddy Fender, a Chicano R&B star in the 1950s and a bilingual country star in the 1970s, joined forces with San Antonio's Doug Sahm, who recorded and performed in countless Texas styles over a 40-year career, and Augie Meyers, Sahm's lifetime collaborator and a versatile keyboardist in his own right, to take an eclectic, infectious Sound of San Antonio around the world. The Tornados weren't the only nowhere-else-but-Texas group to gain an international reputation. Denton's freewheeling "nuclear polka" crew Brave Combo is still going strong after three decades.

The list of Texas country stars is nearly endless. Tex Ritter (Carthage) followed Gene Autry as a singing cowboy. Though Bob Wills and Milton Brown were by far the two biggest western swing bandleaders, during the music's heyday dozens of superb bands such as Cliff Bruner's Texas Wanderers (Houston) and Adolph Hofner's Pearl Wranglers (San Antonio) worked the state. Later Hank Thompson's small-group western swing/honky-tonk fusion yielded countless hits. Houston's Ted Daffan was another bridge between swing and honky-tonk. In addition to Ernest Tubb and Floyd Tillman, Al Dexter (Jacksonville) was there at the birth of the honky-tonk sound, and a flood of Texans led by Lefty Frizzell (Corsicana) and Ray Price (Perryville) soon

Conjunto star Eva Ybarra

followed. Between them and the outlaw era of Willie and
Waylon came singers as diverse as Johnny Horton (Rusk),
Jimmy Dean (Olton), Jeannie C. Riley (Anson), and Tanya
Tucker (Seminole). Kris Kristofferson (Brownsville) was an
outlaw at heart who won crossover and Nashville success. In
the years during and after the peak of outlaw music, Barbara
Mandrell, Gene Watson, Kenny Rogers, and Mickey Gilley

(all Houston), Johnny Rodriguez (Sabinal), and Freddy
Fender rode the country charts. Today the Americana wing
of country is led by the likes of Hayes Carll (The Woodlands),
Rosie Flores and Steve Earle (both San Antonio), Patty
Griffin (Austin), and Ray Wylie Hubbard (Wimberley).
Recent Nashville mainstream country stars rooted in
Texas include the Dixie Chicks (Dallas), Lee Ann Womack
(Jacksonville), and Miranda Lambert (Lindale).

The list of Texans in jazz is equally impressive. Among
the early creators of the music are ragtime pianist Scott
Joplin (Texarkana), guitarist Charlie Christian (Bonham),
and trumpeter Jack Teagarden (Vernon). Other Texans
most worth checking out are swing trombonist/guitarist/
arranger Eddie Durham (San Marcos), swing tenor Herschel
Evans (Denton), swing trumpeter Oran "Hot Lips" Page
(Dallas), swing drummer Gus Johnson (Tyler), bop pianist
Red Garland (Dallas), bop trumpeter Kenny Dorham
(Fairfield), bop bassist Gene Ramey (Austin), and Houston
soul-jazz mainstays The Jazz Crusaders. An entire school
of saxophonists, known as Texas Tenors for their fat,
wide-open sounds, includes Illinois Jacquet, Arnett Cobb,
and Billy Harper from Houston, James Clay and David
"Fathead" Newman from Dallas, Buddy Tate from Sherman,
and Booker Ervin from Denison. The cream of the Texas
avant-garde crop includes Julius Hemphill (Fort Worth)
on alto, Bobby Bradford (Dallas) on trumpet, John Carter

The Dixie Chicks: Emily Robison, Natalie Maines, Martie Maguire

(Fort Worth) on clarinet, Dewey Redman (Fort Worth) on tenor, and Ronald Shannon Jackson (Fort Worth) on drums. Fort Worth's Ornette Coleman is, of course, the undisputed father of them all.

And you know what's most amazing about this much lengthier list? There's still plenty more Texans where they came from who left indelible commercial and artistic marks on American music.

That's what you call an embarrassment of riches.

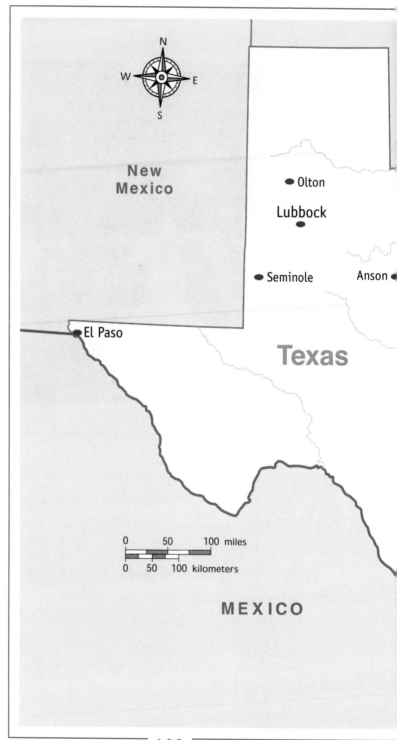

New
Mexico

● Olton

Lubbock
●

● Seminole   Anson ●

● El Paso

Texas

0   50   100 miles

0   50   100 kilometers

MEXICO

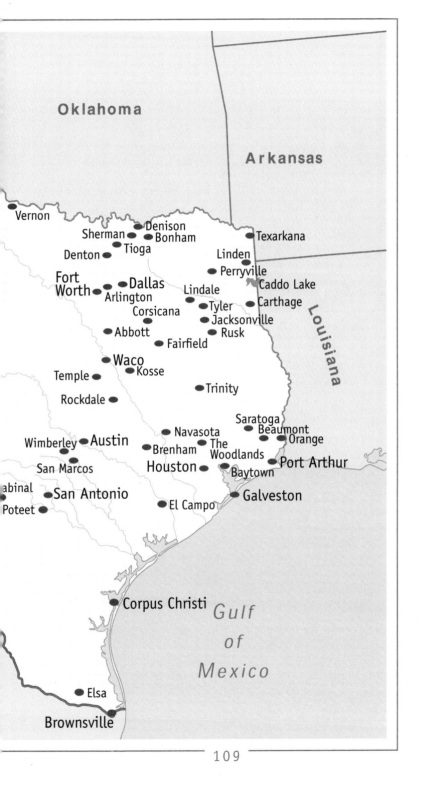

Index

About the author

John Morthland has been writing about music since 1969 when he began working as an associate editor at *Rolling Stone*. He has also been editor of *Creem* and a contributing editor to *Country Music* and *Texas Monthly* magazines. He freelances extensively for other music and general-interest publications and online. He is currently the blues columnist for eMusic.com. Morthland is the author of *The Best of Country Music* and the editor of *Mainlines, Blood Feasts and Bad Taste: A Lester Bangs Reader.* He lives in Austin.